FIND LIGHT IN THE DARKNESS

Five Life Lessons from a Motivational Speaker

IFE THOMAS

TABLE OF CONTENTS

Dear

Keith, Kit and Joseph

You are awesome humans, thank You for shining your lights

YC Thomas

Introduction

As a neurodiverse international TEDx speaker and a motivational speaker for some of the world's biggest organisations, I'm no stranger to sharing my story on a big stage. I'm known for my positivity, my ability to help people transform their lives, and my big smile. I love it when people say that I'm a ray of sunshine because that's exactly what I want to be and how I like to show up in the world. It's how I help other people to show up too.

But the thing that people might not know about me is that in order to shine this brightly, I've had to learn how to sit in a lot of darkness.

Me speaking at the Shine the Light Conference for Autism Awareness

My path to professional success hasn't always been a smooth one. Before I became a speaker and a writer, I was a dancer. I performed on stages with people like Paul McCartney and Leona Lewis and I worked on TV shows like The X-Factor.

A quick photo backstage after the show

It was a life that I loved and one that I'd worked hard to create, so when a knee injury ground my career to a halt, it came as the most crushing disappointment. Later, when I tried to create a new direction for my career by appearing as a housemate on Big Brother, my excitement quickly turned to sadness when I suffered hate and online abuse from people who had never even met me.

Me with Davina McCall during my exit interview for Big Brother

Me entering the Big Brother house

My professional challenges have been more than matched by my personal struggles, which began when, aged just six weeks old, my birth parents vanished from my life. Essentially, I experienced my first rejection before I had even developed the muscles to smile.

My parents were Nigerian and in the UK on student visas when I was born. Once they graduated, their visas ran out and they had to return to Nigeria – and they chose not to take me with them. They wanted me to stay in the UK so that I could gain British citizenship. Having spoken to my birth mother about this recently, I know what an enormously difficult decision this was for them to make. They did it because they wanted me to grow up with all the opportunities that living in the UK could bring.

Fortunately, my birth parents helped to find a wonderful family to adopt me – a family who gave me all the love a child could ever need. I'm hugely grateful for the childhood I was given, but I'd be lying if I said that growing up as a black child with white parents in 1980s Newport Pagnell was easy. Dealing with other people's attitudes was a daily struggle that I needed to overcome.

Life for me became even more complicated when I realised from an early age that I felt different from my childhood friends and I didn't experience life in the same way.

I never enjoyed playing with toys or going to sleepovers, and I never, ever understood jokes. As life went on, the distance I felt between myself and other people only seemed to grow, and it blighted my life in so many ways. It wasn't until I was an adult that I was diagnosed with autism, which explained the sense of alienation I'd felt all my life.

But autism hasn't just affected my life. Before I received my own diagnosis, my eldest son was diagnosed with autism aged two. To be told that your beautiful toddler may never achieve anything in his life is one of the most shocking things I've ever experienced. The worry was overwhelming.

There's no doubt that I've been through a lot of darkness in my life – but what I've learned is that the times I've sat in the darkness have been the moments that have made me. I believe that when you are in the darkness it gives you time to develop – just like a photograph. The darkness always gives you the opportunity to think things through, work things out, and start to gain clarity. Slowly, just like that photograph, everything will begin to come sharply into focus. Before you know it, you will have developed your resilience, your strength and your mindset and you'll be ready to get out there on display again.

As a personal development expert, I've spent years studying psychology, philosophy, quantum physics theory and neuroscience. Over the years this knowledge has helped me to develop a failsafe five-step plan that has ALWAYS managed to take me from a place of darkness to a place of light

… and I've written this book to share it with you. It's my own recipe for success, and if you follow every step, it's guaranteed to work.

Each chapter of this book features a story from my life followed by one of my five practical, actionable steps that you can apply to your own life. They are:

1. **Decide what you want**
2. **Find someone to help you**
3. **Take control of your thoughts**
4. **Reinvent yourself by creating a powerful personality**
5. **Never give up**

Whether you are facing your own specific challenges or you're on a personal development mission to become the very best version of yourself, I want you to see this book as your handbook to success.

I can show you how to use the darkness to your advantage and turn your pain into power. I can help you ensure that nothing ever dims your light. Sound good? Okay. It's time to get started.

CHAPTER 1:

Finding the light when your plans for the future crumble

When I think about the moment when all my dreams for the future crumbled, the thing that stands out the most to me is the sound of a horrendous crunch. As soon as I heard it, I just knew that everything I had worked so hard for was over.

When I first stepped into the dance studio that day, I was in my happy place. I remember how confident I felt. I'd learned the choreography, I'd put on my heels, and as soon as the music started, I began moving, grooving and living my best life. I just knew that I could get this gig.

In front of me was a panel of producers who were auditioning me to star in a TV advert for a major drinks brand. Not only was this job going to be well paid, but it also involved travelling to Argentina and dancing alongside Pharrell Williams – a singer that I'd been a fan of for years.

Talk about a dream job. It felt like it could be the cumulation of everything I had been working so hard for. I was 28 years old and I'd been dancing since I was nine. I'd studied dance at the prestigious Urdang Academy where I'd poured blood, sweat and tears into becoming a success. After that, I'd danced on the West End stage and on TV shows like The X-Factor.

I'd always known that dance wouldn't be a long-term career option so, as time had gone on and I'd become older, I'd begun to diversify my career opportunities. I had joined a girl pop group and enjoyed a stint on reality TV.

More recently, I had set up a business called the National Network of Chartered Accountants. The business was going really well and it was growing very quickly – I'd moved into an office and employed a team of people. However you looked at it, I'd made the venture into a success, but I couldn't help feeling that this corporate work wasn't very 'me'. Dancing had always been my first love so when I'd received a call about this audition, I had jumped at it. If I got this job, I knew that it would give me the opportunity to take my dancing to the next level and to get my name out there to even more people. It felt like it could be my last real chance to show the world what I was capable of. I wanted it so badly.

My dance routine was going well. I was so well practised that muscle memory had kicked in and I could just relax and enjoy myself. I smiled broadly as I pictured myself dancing in the golden Buenos Aires sun next to Pharell, and the members of the audition panel smiled back at me.

Then came the moment in my routine for the big kick. I threw one leg up in the air, just like I'd rehearsed. But, in that moment, I heard a horrific crunch from my standing leg as my knee completely gave way.

After that, everything seemed to happen in slow motion. As I crashed down to the ground, I could feel my hopes and dreams coming crashing down with me. Gripped by panic, I tried to stand up again, but I realised that I simply wasn't able to – my knee just couldn't take any weight. By this point, I could feel tears of disappointment starting to sting my eyes and I was desperate to get myself out of view of the panel. I found myself shuffling across the floor on my backside. And just when I thought things couldn't possibly get any worse, I looked up and saw one of the producers take his pen and draw a line on the piece of paper in front of him. He was crossing my name off the audition list while I was still scooting off the stage and wincing in pain!

I somehow managed to limp my way home that day. Things felt bleak because I'd missed my opportunity to perform in the advert with Pharell but perhaps, I thought, my knee could be fixed. Perhaps I'd be back to dancing and auditioning again soon. Perhaps this wasn't the end. After all, I reasoned, I'd had issues with this knee for years and I'd always come back from them.

My knee troubles all stemmed from an incident in a dancing lesson back when I was 16 years old. I did a box split jump and a fellow student crashed into my leg while they were doing a kick of their own. The impact of the collision over-extended my knee. When I went to see the doctor about it at the time, he didn't seem particularly worried – he just gave me some crutches, told me to rest, and sent me on my way. If he wasn't worried then I figured that I didn't need to worry either. Sure enough, my knee got better in the short term, but as the years went on it seemed to become increasingly weak and it gave way regularly.

At the Urdang, I found myself choreographing routines that allowed me to avoid any moves that would put too much strain on that knee. I hid the fact that I had an injury and I even switched from doing ballet and contemporary dance to doing commercial dance as I knew that would be easier on my injury. Dance was my life and I had done everything in my power to become a success in the dance world. I couldn't let what had happened at this audition set me back. Maybe all I needed was a little bit of rest.

My brother-in-law was an osteopath so, once I arrived home from the audition, I called him to ask for his advice. He told me that my knee needed an MRI scan so I booked one straight away.

Any hope that I had held onto quickly seeped away as the doctors broke the news to me about the results of my scan. I had snapped my anterior cruciate ligament (ACL) during my audition. They told me that there was a lot of scar tissue on my ACL as a result of my earlier injury. They said that it had been hanging on by a thread, but the kick at the audition had been the last straw that caused the whole thing to tear.

I had keyhole surgery on my knee. I remember the moment when I came around from surgery, still groggy with the anaesthetic.

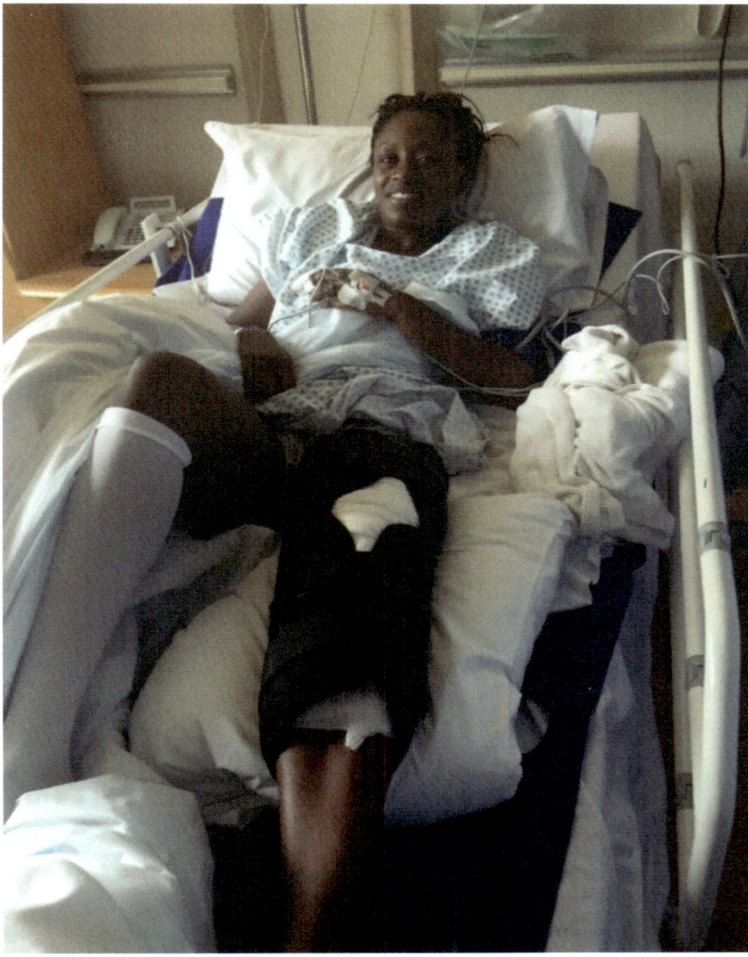

I knew that I should have felt happy that the doctors had done their best to fix my knee, but instead I was overwhelmed with anger. It all seemed too little too late. Why hadn't I been sent for an MRI when I'd suffered my original injury? Why had I just been left to get on with things and allowed to dance on that knee over and over again to the extent that my ACL snapped during an audition? What would I have been able to achieve in my dance career if I'd been able to get the medical support that I'd needed back when I was 16?

I'd spent so many years trying to live with my knee injury and compensate for it rather than truly flourishing as a dancer. I couldn't help but feel that

I'd been robbed of the opportunity to show the world just how well I could dance because I'd never had the physical ability to do so. It made me furious.

Some dancers are able to return to their careers following ACL surgery if they have the time available to do the rehab and train around the clock. But I was very aware that I wasn't a dance student anymore. I was 28 years old, I was the mother of two young boys and I was running my own business. My work and family responsibilities meant that I wasn't able to spend every moment concentrating on my dancing. I simply didn't have the time to devote months and months to rehabilitating my knee and getting back into dancing shape to the exclusion of everything else. It just wasn't going to happen.

As I sat there, dazed in my checked hospital gown, a darkness descended upon me. I knew then that my dance career was over and I was engulfed by a huge sense of loss. I had been through a lot in my life, but knowing that all of my hopes for the career that I loved lay in tatters was almost too much to bear.

It was one of the darkest moments of my life. Dancing had been my everything and now it felt like there was nothing. I had my own business, but my heart wasn't in it anymore. I felt like I had no idea how to move forward. What was I going to do with my life now?

In that little hospital room I sat alone with my darkness. I sat with it and I meditated on it. Giving up was not an option – I had two boys who were relying on me to provide for them. I needed financial independence.

All of a sudden, it occurred to me that I had been a good dancer despite my injury because I had put my mind to it and given it everything I had. I had created a successful business despite it being in an area outside of my experience because I had put my mind to that too. I realised that if I applied the same principle to any other career and I truly threw myself into it then I would be able to achieve the same results.

I realised that it was time to be brave, to step out of my comfort zone and to try something new – something that I would love and something that I could thrive in. To begin with, I signed up for a course by the inspirational American coach Marie Forleo about how to create a career you love, and I decided to give it my all. So that's exactly what I did.

I learned a lot from that course and my eyes were opened to so many new possibilities. After that, I studied with the legendary self-development expert Brian Tracy and learned all of his techniques and strategies for business success. I soaked in everything he said and hung on his every word – and most importantly, I translated everything into action and remained persistent. Before long, I realised that I had a gift for coaching people and helping them to achieve their dreams. Off the back of this, I began working with clients and had nothing but success. I then wrote my own book and created an online course – both of which have gone on to help hundreds and thousands of people to reach their goals.

Writing my first book was just the beginning for me

I'm now considered a thought leader in the world of personal development and I'm a sought-after motivational speaker for some of the world's biggest organisations as well as being an international TEDx speaker.

I talk on subjects such as business, sales and marketing, personal development, autism and conscious parenting.

When my dance career ended, it was devastating. But what I discovered was that by allowing myself to sit in that darkness, I soon saw the light. I realised that when something doesn't go to plan in life, you have to see it as an opportunity to grow and adapt by trying something new and stretch yourself in a way that shows you what you are capable of.

I've had many careers and none of them have been instant successes. But I've got to where I am today through hard work and persistence. When things have gone wrong, I've spent time working out the way forward – because there is always a way forward.

One of my favourite Oprah Winfrey quotes that I say to myself often is, "Ask yourself, what is the next right step?"

The idea behind this quote is to break down challenges into manageable actions. Instead of becoming overwhelmed by the entirety of a task or a journey, focus on the next immediate action you can take that aligns with your truth and values.

Whenever I'm doing something that isn't working, I force myself to be brave and to pivot. I am always open to changing my plans based on new information. Whatever happens, I keep going. I've discovered that there's nothing wrong with pivoting – in fact some people call me the Princess of the Pivot!

When I'm not sure what to do in a new endeavour, I search for an expert and follow their advice. And, most importantly, when I decide to do something, I go all in and give it everything I've got. And if I can do all of these things, then you can too.

LIFE LESSON 1:

Decide what you want

Whether you need to start all over again, just like I did, whether there's something you've always wanted to achieve but you're not sure how to get there, or whether you're simply feeling stuck in your life, this exercise will help.

Think big – then think bigger!

One of the things that can set people back in knowing what they want to do with their lives is fear. They worry about failing. They worry about setting goals that are unrealistic. They set their sights too low. I'm here to tell you not to do that. Now is not the time for modesty – now is the time to be audacious! What's the thing you want that will allow you to live out the truest, highest expression of who you are? What is the burning desire that's always been inside you? What would you dare to dream if you knew you couldn't fail?

For example, if you've always wanted to write a screenplay, why stop there? Why not aim to win an Oscar with it? Don't be shy about it. Don't think it's silly. Own it. One of my biggest goals is to collaborate with Oprah Winfrey, so I own it and I put it out there. I've no doubt that one day I will achieve it.

Get laser focussed.

When we're working to build the life of our dreams, we're going to have lots of goals. That's exactly how it should be. But, here's the crucial thing you need to know if you want to be successful: you should only work on one goal at a time.

Here's a simple task to make sure that you're laser focussed about what you want to achieve and you're putting your time and energy in the right place. If you want results, don't be tempted to skip it!

- Grab a pen and a piece of paper.

- Write down the ten things that you really want to achieve – and be specific.
- Look at your list and circle the one goal that would have the biggest impact on your life right now. Be honest about it.

Once you've selected your goal, it's an absolute game changer, because you now know exactly where you need to focus your efforts and you can start building your roadmap to reach it. And how do you do that? Check out the next Life Lesson in Chapter 2.

CHAPTER 2:

Finding the light when you've lost your way.

It was 2010 and I was standing excitedly behind a huge pair of double doors in one of the most famous houses in the world. I was waiting for them to open so that I could step out into the limelight and begin the next chapter of my life. I had butterflies in my tummy. Then, as the doors slowly began to part, I heard that undeniable sound of a chorus of boos and the butterflies quickly turned to an aching feeling.

I had applied for a place on the 11th season of Big Brother because, given my knee problems, I knew that the time was ticking on my dance career. I felt that appearing on the UK's most popular reality show would build my profile and take things to the next level. I also thought it would be a lot of fun. When I got the phone call that summer to say that I'd been chosen to be one of the housemates, I was ecstatic. I was sworn to secrecy and wasn't able to tell anyone about it, and I was excited to see where this one-of-a-kind opportunity would take me.

I had lots of fun on top secret shopping trips where I picked out outfits to take with me. But it wasn't just clothes that I took in my suitcase. I also took along a selection of wigs to wear during my stay. Determined to be my authentic self and embrace every facet of my identity, I became one of the first black females on the show to openly change their wigs. In an act of raw authenticity, I even shaved my head live on national television. It wasn't about making a statement; it was about showing up as myself – unapologetically and confidently. My journey resonated with many people, particularly those battling cancer. So many people reached out to me to express how seeing me change my hair and wigs gave them confidence.

I had a great time on the show, just like I'd hoped that I would. I met so many people from different walks of life. Generally I got on with everyone but, of course there were a few arguments. It wouldn't be Big Brother without a bit of drama, after all! I took part in all sorts of silly challenges and had some bizarre and wonderful experiences that I'll never have again. Someone reminded me recently that I once dined in the sky during my time on the show, and that I also dressed up as a superhero. My superpower was astonishing strength!

It was an exhilarating time in my life and it all seemed to whiz by in a blur. I was always aware that the cameras were watching me, but whatever happened, I had resolved to stay true to myself, regardless of how I might be portrayed, so that's exactly what I did.

When I was the fifth person to be evicted from the house after 38 days, I was a little disappointed that I hadn't made it further in the competition, but I felt like I'd achieved what I'd gone on the show to achieve – to show the UK who Ife Thomas was. I also missed my loved ones massively and was desperate to get back home to them for a joyous celebration.

Unfortunately it didn't work out quite like that.

As the doors opened and I heard the crowd's boos, it occurred to me that perhaps the UK didn't like who Ife Thomas was. My heart plummeted and I felt a sense of humiliation begin to rise up inside me. However, being the professional that I was, I plastered a broad smile on my face, waved to the audience and descended the famous steps to pose for the cameras.

After that, Davina McCall, the show's host, took me for my exit interview during which the sheer magnitude of what I'd just experienced started to hit me. Being under such an intense spotlight and being vulnerable to public judgement and scrutiny suddenly felt frightening.

I remember that once the interview came to an end, I sat on my own and the darkness began to creep in. I felt like people didn't like me and I wondered where I had gone wrong. All I had done was be myself. I wondered if going into the Big Brother house had been a huge mistake. What if rather than build my profile appearing on the show had actually destroyed it? I felt lost and alone.

But that's when I saw Chrissy heading over to me with her arms outstretched.

Chrissy is my best friend in the whole world. But as well as being my best friend, she's also my mentor and my guiding light. Chrissy is a world-class singer and singing teacher with the most beautiful voice. She's recorded everything from opera to rock songs and she's appeared on more TV shows and stages than it's possible to count. What she doesn't know about showbiz simply isn't worth knowing.

I've known Chrissy for years – ever since we both reached for the same copy of The Stage newspaper in a branch of WH Smith in 2005. The stars must have aligned that fateful day, because it was a wonderful chance meeting that changed my life forever. We started chatting about the entertainment world right there in front of the newspapers, and we haven't really stopped since.

Apart from my husband Terrence and my elder sister Mandy, Chrissy is the person who knows me better than anyone else.

After I came out of the Big Brother house, I was full of emotions. Chrissy could intuitively tell that I was beginning to doubt myself and beginning to wobble. She knew that all I wanted to do at that moment was run away and hide. However, as a straight-talking northerner, Chrissy wasn't having any of it.

"Ife," she said as she held my hands and looked me dead in the eye. "You are not in control of how people edit you, but you are in control of how you manage this moment right here, right now. You are not going to hide away. You are going to capitalise on this moment to push your career forwards, and you're not going to let any of those haters make you sad."

It was a transformative moment for me. I knew that Chrissy was right, and I knew that I needed to remember who I was and take control of my own narrative.

"You know," she added. "The problem with opinions is that they are like arseholes: everybody's got one, but you don't necessarily want to acquaint yourself with them all!"

For the first time since my eviction, I collapsed into a fit of giggles. After that, I pulled myself together and headed off into the night to talk to the press with Chrissy by my side, ready to step back into my power.

And that wasn't the first time that Chrissy's knowledge and expertise has played a crucial role in helping me to step out of the darkness and into the light.

Shortly before my stint on Big Brother, I had set up a girl group. I recruited three other female singers and together we grafted, working on songs and dance routines. We were all hungry to make it and become one of the big girl bands at the time alongside the likes of Girls Aloud, The Saturdays and The Pussycat Dolls. I was the driving force in the project, putting a lot of my own money into the group and using my contacts to get us meetings within the industry.

It was early days, but things were looking good. I was convinced that we were on the brink of being signed to a major label, so I was devastated the day I was told that not only had the other three members of the group left me to go it alone, but they had also used my contacts to do it. It felt like the most enormous betrayal imaginable.

The experience left me feeling broken, but Chrissy was there to help me pick up the pieces. Like me, she was furious with the other members of the group for their conduct, but she told me that I mustn't let it bring me down. She told me to hold my head up high and use that disappointment as fuel to keep pushing forwards, so that's what I did.

The girl group never made it big after they left me, but several years later, one of the members went on to find success as a singer and TV presenter. Now that she's a household name, she always pops up on the TV and, for the longest time I'd feel angry whenever I saw her. But in recent years I've done the work to put that sense of betrayal behind me. Chrissy has helped me with that too.

What I've discovered through my friendship with Chrissy is how valuable it is to have someone with knowledge and experience to help you as you work towards your goals. My goals at that time were all related to the entertainment industry, and Chrissy was able to guide me through and advise me every step of the way.

Without Chrissy's support, I might have settled for second best. I might have let people take advantage of my hunger and enthusiasm and performed for the minimum wage. I might have lost my confidence and walked away from the industry entirely. But Chrissy didn't let me. She built up my resilience, boosted my self-esteem and showed me how to deal with the business side of things and make sure I never lost my way.

Over the years I have changed careers and started a family, but Chrissy has continued to support me every step of the way. Whenever I'm going through a difficult time, she's the first person I call because she always helps me to look at the bigger picture – and just as importantly, to make me laugh. I believe that everybody needs to find their own Chrissy.

LIFE LESSON 2:

Surround yourself with people who can help you get to where you want to be

It has taken me many years to understand that if you want to win in life, you can't do it alone. When you know what you want to achieve, you'll get there a whole lot quicker with help and support from the right people. Success never takes a linear path, so no matter how motivated, skilled or confident you are, you're still likely to come up against stumbling blocks where you'll need advice or low moments where you'll need cheering on. That's where your advisor and your A-Team come in.

Find your advisor

Whenever you're going somewhere new in your car, you use your satnav to get a clear map of the most direct route. The satnav's expertise means you get to where you want to be quickly and effectively and you avoid wasting any time driving around aimlessly. Well, when you're trying to reach a goal in life, you need to do exactly the same thing. And how do you do that? Simple. You find someone who has achieved what you want to achieve, or had helped someone get where you want to be. You ask them how they got there and then – most importantly – you follow the direction you have been given. Here's how to do it:

Step 1:

Identify up to five people who have done the thing that you want to do. The more people you speak to, the more advice you'll receive, which means you'll have more information to work from.

Step 2:

Ask your experts what they had to do to get where they are. Approaching people to ask for advice may sound intimidating, but people who have worked hard to achieve success are usually very happy to share their story and pass on their expertise. You might get the answers you need by sending a polite email, making a respectful phone call, or offering to buy someone a coffee. You might even learn what you need to know by reading a book that your expert has written, taking a course that they run, or hiring them as a coach.

Step 3:

Look at the information you have gathered from your experts and break down the steps they took to get to where they are. Make it into your own personal road map. Give yourself a deadline for reaching each step on the journey … and then get started! One of my favourite questions to ask them is, "What would you do differently if you were to start again in today's landscape?"

Assemble your A-Team

I believe that every successful person who has ever achieved anything in life has a support network. For me, I have Chrissy, along with my family, friends, advisors, coaches and mentors.

Every triumph, every milestone achieved in life, can often be traced back to the support system that stands firmly behind the achiever. This unwavering support network isn't just family or friends but extends to advisors, coaches, mentors, and for some, spiritual guides. In my life, Chrissy stands tall alongside a band of individuals who've guided me through thick and thin.

My journey with Terrance, my partner of nearly two decades, has been filled with love, learning, and shared dreams. While we had built a life brimming with shared accomplishments, one crucial decision remained pending: marriage. The idea of tying the knot was tinged with spiritual uncertainty. How could I, a devout Christian, align my life under the eyes of God with Terrance, an agnostic who leaned more towards evidence and science than faith?

It was during this period of contemplation that I sought the counsel of two individuals who have grown into the roles of my spiritual compass: my pastor and the first lady. Their insight wasn't just about religious doctrine but a deeper understanding of love, commitment, and life itself. They reminded me of the life Terrance and I had already built, the love we shared, and the commitment that had already stood the test of time.

(Guided by Spiritual Leaders)

Every soul yearns for guidance, a voice of reason and wisdom. Terrance and I found this solace in Andrea and Phil, our spiritual leaders who have been our guiding lights since 2016. Their presence in our lives hasn't been about imposing a doctrine but providing understanding, wisdom, and a perspective shaped by faith and love.

The day Terrance and I decided to make our union official, it was Andrea and Phil who stood by our side, bearing witness to our vows. Their role wasn't just ceremonial; it was a commitment from their side to be our guiding stars. As witnesses to our union, they pledged to be our pillars of strength, our spiritual touchstones, keeping us rooted in the principles that first brought us together.

In life, we find various people playing distinct roles. While some offer love, others provide wisdom, guidance, or mentorship. But among these, having spiritual leaders like Andrea and Phil is a blessing. They don't just guide us in times of spiritual uncertainty but hold us accountable to our commitments, reminding us continually of the sanctity and essence of the vows we've made.

The motivational speaker Jim Rohm once famously said, "You are the average of the five people you spend the most time with".

He said that if you hang around with people who are doing nothing with their lives, you will end up doing nothing with yours. Before you know it, you will start to think the same as them, earn the same as them and, ultimately, live your life in the same way as them. Les Brown, another motivational speaker, pointed out that if you're around cynical and negative people all the time, you will become cynical and negative too.

I believe them. I also believe that if you want to succeed in achieving your goals then you need to surround yourself with people who encourage, influence, educate and inspire you to be more than you think you can be. These are the people who will stand by you in your darkest hour. These are the people who will reach out their hands to you and pull you up when you hit rock bottom. These are the people who will cheer you on and keep you going whenever you are on the verge of quitting. These are the people you need in your A-Team.

So, whatever your goal, I want you to spend some time looking at the people you spend most of your time with and ask yourself whether they will support you to achieve it. If they aren't helping you to grow mentally, emotionally or spiritually, then perhaps it's time to spend less time with them and concentrate on assembling your A-Team instead.

CHAPTER 3:

Finding the light when you've been written off

Throughout my entire life, people have made assumptions about me and written me off. Whether it's because I'm female, because I'm black, because I'm adopted, or because I worked in entertainment, I've always had to work hard to overcome prejudice. It's become second nature to me.

Over the years, I've learned how to deal with brush offs and put downs by developing a rock solid sense of self-confidence. These days, no matter what anybody says to me, nothing can shake my belief in the fact that I am somebody. It wasn't until I started my family that I realised I could help others by telling them how to develop their self-confidence too.

It all started when my first son was born. Like any new parents, my husband Terrence and I were delighted to have this gorgeous little bundle of joy in our lives. Quincy was such a cute, happy baby and we were completely and utterly wrapped up in him. A year later, our second son, Quba, arrived and our family was complete. Life with two young boys was a crazy, wonderful blur.

As Quincy grew, we began to realise that he was different from his peers as he didn't want to speak to anybody and he would scream when we went into shops. When he was two years old, we took him to the hospital to meet with a paediatrician, an educational psychologist, and a speech and language therapist. After observing Quincy for some time, they sat Terrence and I down and said, "We're sorry to inform you that Quincy has autism spectrum disorder and he is going to struggle for the rest of his life".

We were told that all the things that we'd hoped that Quincy would be able to have – a good education, a great career and an independent life – we would have to shelf. I remember sitting in that office feeling so scared, afraid, lost and overwhelmed.

When we went home, we cried and we grieved. I had so many questions so, desperate to find the answers, I turned to Google. I found some horrible statistics on the National Autism Society's website that said people with autism are 28 times more likely to take their own lives. It's one of the worst things that a parent could possibly read.

I signed up for lots of events and workshops for parents with autistic children. I found myself at one where they were showing us how to restrain our children. They were talking about how we needed to put headgear on them to protect them if they were having a meltdown or an epileptic fit.

Everything just felt so bleak. And it didn't help that when I told people about Quincy's autism diagnosis some people responded by saying, "Oh, poor you. That's a shame. But at least you've got another son".

Later, when Quincy started school, the headteacher told me in no uncertain terms that there was no way in which Quincy would ever have the ability to sit his SATS or his GCSEs.

"It's just the way it is, Mrs Thomas," she said.

When I looked at my son, I saw a beautiful, happy little boy who was extremely talented in art and animation. There was so much to celebrate, and yet I was constantly being told by medical professionals, the school system and even friends and family that he would never amount to anything. It didn't make sense to me. What's more, I worried that if people were saying these things to me, what were people going to say to him? I worried that if he was being written off all the time, the effect on his self-esteem could be catastrophic.

I found myself wondering, "Why aren't there any success stories? Why can't I find anyone to tell me the great things about autism?"

I kept searching for autistic boys, men or people who were successful – people who didn't see autism as a life sentence – but I couldn't find anyone. I couldn't find anything to tell me that Quincy was going to be okay. It was so frightening.

But, one thing I did notice when I was reading all the literature was that autistic people often lack self-confidence and self-esteem, and that this can have a huge impact on their mental health. A person with autism is more likely to have suicidal thoughts and depression than the rest of the population, so I started thinking about what I could do to help counterbalance that and prevent my child from becoming a statistic.

And then I thought about everything that I'd trained myself to do over the years to defy people's expectations and overcome their prejudices. Through my work in the world of personal development, one of the main things I've learned is that success generally all boils down to the power that comes from the words we say to ourselves.

I felt that if I could teach Quincy how to like himself and believe in himself, that would be the greatest legacy I possibly leave. For him, it would mean a strong foundation that he could build the rest of his life on, and for me it would mean peace of mind. It would mean knowing that he was not going to take his own life.

So, I developed four positive and powerful affirmations for Quincy to say to himself every single day. They were:

"I am somebody. I am good enough. I can do anything. I like myself."

I started trying to get him to say the words whilst looking at himself in the mirror, but he wouldn't do that. That's when I hit upon the idea of printing those words onto a mirror and asking him to read them that way.

That's how The Confidence Star was born – a star-shaped mirror featuring the affirmations. I like to think of it as my gift to the world.

By reading the words, Quincy wasn't consciously aware that he was looking at himself, but there's a power when you speak to yourself in the mirror. There have been lots of books written about positive affirmations, and scientific studies that show how they can change the neural pathways in the brain. There's so much evidence to back it up but, as a mum, I was just desperate to ensure my son believed in himself.

After watching him read the affirmations every day, I saw the confidence grow in him. I saw his development from a little boy who didn't like to speak, to a boy who was relaxing into himself, smiling and laughing. It was astonishing.

What's more, other parents saw that change in him too. They started to ask me about the positive words that Quincy was saying to himself, because they wanted to use them to help their children as well. When I told them about The Confidence Star, it soon became obvious that this was a product that parents wanted. After all, doesn't every mother and every father want their child to like and believe in themselves?

Me delivering a Confidence Star workshop to parents

Now, The Confidence Star is in homes, schools, hospitals, nurseries and so many other places all around the world. Children use it, adults use it, and the feedback that I get about it honestly takes my breath away. People say that it has changed their lives for the better. They say that they now understand the power of the words they say to themselves.

I like to think of The Confidence Star as anti-viral software for the mind. It's something that you can install every single day and it will protect you from any outside criticism as well as your own internal criticism. It's preventative, it's proactive and it's reactive.

CLARITY
COURAGE
CONSISTENCY
OWN
MINDWORKOUT

As for Quincy, he's now a confident self-assured joyful twelve-year-old boy who is absolutely crushing life. Not only did he take his SATS, but he got the most incredible results and rose to the top amongst many of his peers in his fantastic mainstream school. Outside of school, he loves to work on his own animation projects and has got his sights firmly set on doing it professionally – and there's absolutely no reason why he shouldn't be able to. By developing his self-confidence he has proven every single person who doubted him wrong and I couldn't be prouder.

LIFE LESSON 3:

Take control of your thoughts

When it comes to achieving your goals, your mindset is everything. I truly believe that you can have all the strategy, drive and passion in the world, but if you don't have a positive mindset and unshakable self-confidence, then then you won't be able to achieve the things you want to achieve.

And why's that? Well, whenever we're working towards anything we often have to deal with knocks and setbacks or being written off – it's par for the course. And it can be so easy to let these things derail us and prevent us from reaching our goals. It can be easy to start to think we're not good enough and that we should abandon our hopes and dreams. But, if you are confident and you believe in yourself, then you're so much more likely to be able to bounce back from anything that life throws at you.

People often tell me that they envy my confidence and say they wished they could be more like me. And the thing I tell them is that they CAN be. It's simple – it just takes commitment. Here are some ways to do it.

Manage your mindset

The only difference between you and the people who are where you want to be is that they have learned how to think differently. They are able to take control of their thoughts and focus all their energy on getting what they really want. But the great news is that this way of thinking isn't just reserved for Olympic athletes and tech billionaires – it's something that YOU can learn to do too.

The fact of the matter is, your thoughts can make you or break you. They can affect every aspect of your life. It may sound obvious, but what I've discovered is that the more positive thoughts we have, the more good things we see in life, the more positive we become, and the more likely we are to get to where we want to be. And, conversely, the more negative thoughts we have, the more bad things we see, the more negative we become, and the less likely we are to become a winner.

So many of us go through our lives assuming that we are slaves to our negative thoughts and powerless against them. But the thing is, we really can change our thoughts and take complete control of them – it all just comes down to self-awareness.

Flip the script

The key to creating a winning mindset involves monitoring your thoughts carefully and then turning every negative thought into a positive one. This this little exercise can help you do it:

- The next time a negative thought pops up in your head – no matter whether it's about yourself, someone else or a situation you're in – simply notice it and pause.
- Decide to get rid of that thought – choose to push it out of your brain. This takes real focus, so what I suggest you do is verbalise it and shout, "Out!"
- Once you've let go of a negative thought, it's time to replace it with something positive. For example, if you were thinking negatively about a situation that you find yourself in, start to consider what you can do to turn it around or take back control. If you were thinking negatively about a person, use all the strength you can muster to think of that person with empathy or compassion.

Repeat this exercise again and again and I guarantee that it will soon become a habit. Before you know it, you'll be approaching the world in a completely different way.

Reprogram the way you speak to yourself

Dr. Nathaniel Branden says that your self-esteem is your reputation with yourself, and I totally agree. Confidence all comes down to how you talk about yourself and how you think about yourself. The fact is, if you regularly have negative thoughts about yourself, then you're unlikely to feel very confident.

But you can change all this by simply reprogramming the way you think and speak about yourself. You just need to change up the language and make sure the words you are using are congruent with the person that you want to be. To do this, it's important to get into the habit of saying positive words about yourself every single day.

You might think that speaking positively to yourself and using the affirmations from The Confidence Star sounds silly, but I promise that it's not. It couldn't be more serious. You see, the affirmations get stored in your subconscious mind and work to protect you from both outside criticism and your own internal criticism.

So, here is a task for you for the next week. Every morning, just after you have woken up, go to your nearest mirror, look yourself in the eye and say the following words:

"I am somebody. I am good enough. I can do anything. I like myself."

Don't skip it, don't mumble it – speak to yourself loudly and proudly every morning and, trust me, you will be amazed at the difference it makes. Before you know it, you're going to believe in yourself, you're going to achieve your goals and, quite simply, you're going to be on fire!

CHAPTER 4:

Finding the light when you feel different

Ever since I can remember, I've always felt different to other people. When I was a young child I struggled to understand why other kids enjoyed playing with toys, because I always hated it. My mum would buy Barbies for myself and my younger sister, and I just didn't know what to do with them. My sister would sit happily for hours, completely engrossed in a world of imagination, but it was a place I simply didn't know how to enter. How could I know where Barbie wanted to go or what Barbie wanted to say if I didn't know what Barbie was thinking? It just didn't make any sense to me.

Throughout my childhood I found it extremely difficult to understand social cues, I never 'got' jokes, and I found it really hard to fit in. I always thought there was something wrong with me. I now know that the reason I've always struggled to figure out the world is because I am autistic.

I received my autism diagnosis when I was 30 years old – two years after my son Quincy had received his own diagnosis.

When I was told that I was autistic, I initially felt relief because all of the feelings of alienation that I'd experienced throughout my life suddenly made sense. But soon afterwards, that sense of relief was drowned out by an enormous sense of anger. Why had it taken 30 years for somebody to tell me that there was nothing wrong with me and that my feelings of displacement were the result of me having autistic spectrum disorder (ASD)? Why had I had to endure years of upset and confusion? Years of other people judging me for my 'different' behaviour? Years of expending copious amounts of energy desperately trying to act 'normal'?

It's always better to receive an autism diagnosis as a child, because that gives you more time to implement the coping strategies that you need, however it's very common for women to receive their diagnoses in adulthood. This is because traditional diagnostic criteria for autism were based on research primarily involving boys and, as a result, the signs of autism in girls are often overlooked or misinterpreted. Often girls with autism fly under the radar and are simply dismissed as difficult, disruptive, shy, reclusive or anxious. In my case I was seen as a drama queen.

Growing up with undiagnosed autism affected my life in so many ways. One of these was the fact that I was never very good at dealing with change. A simple change of plans – the sort of thing that other people wouldn't bat an eyelid over – could send me spiralling out of control and end in suicidal thoughts. I found each incident scary, confusing and isolating – but I never had the words to articulate it.

The first time things really came to a head was when I tried to take my own life on a primary school trip to an outdoor activity centre. I was just ten years old. I was really looking forward to going away with my friends. We had an itinerary of what we were doing each day, and I knew that first up was bike riding. I turned up that morning wearing my brand new Reebok trainers – they were ideal for a spin on a bike, I thought. I had been through the bike riding route in my head the night before, so I was feeling very prepared.

Unfortunately, I discovered that my preparations had been in vain when our teacher, Mrs. McGee, announced there had been a change of plans. She said that we were no longer going bike riding – we were going orienteering instead. I froze. Orienteering meant running through the woods. It meant not knowing the route. It meant getting my new trainers dirty. I panicked.

"Why did the plans change?" I asked.

Mrs McGee looked at me, rolled her eyes and told me not to interrupt. She just considered me to be 'the loud kid'. But I needed to know, so I asked again.

"Because they have," she snapped.

I couldn't handle it. It wasn't just the fact that the plans had changed that upset me – it was the fact that I hadn't been given an explanation as to why. And then there was the thought of getting my new trainers muddy when I had planned my outfit so carefully. It was all too much. But what really didn't compute was the fact that when I looked around at the other kids on the trip, nobody else seemed to be worried about the new itinerary at all. Everyone was just taking it in their stride.

I turned around and ran inside to the little dorm that I was sharing with my best friend Jemma. My heart was racing and my breath was shallow. I slammed the door shut behind me, grabbed a wire coat hanger out of the wardrobe, and I put it over my head and around my neck. I frantically started twisting the wire around and round, desperately trying to strangle myself.

A few moments later, Jemma came into the room and when she saw what I was doing, she looked shocked. She ran over to me, grabbing the coat hanger and trying to remove it from my neck while I tried to stop her.

"Stop it, Ife!" she shouted.

"No!" I shouted back through the tears that had just started streaming down my face. "This all makes me so mad! I just can't do this anymore – it's too much for me."

Jemma looked confused and worried as we continued to wrestle over the coat hanger. My tears were coming thick and fast and I couldn't fight anymore. We collapsed into a heap on the floor, me with marks on my neck, Jemma with her arms around my shoulders, trying to comfort me.

There and then in that little dorm room, everything felt so impossible. I had nothing left to give, so I just wanted to give up. I was really struggling to cope with the outside world. These days I'd describe that feeling as my social battery running low, but back then I simply didn't have the words.

Increasingly, people in my life were looking at me like I was a problem. The teachers thought, "This kid is a diva – she thinks she's a star. She's not willing to comply."

Mrs. McGee rang my mum and told her that I was being disruptive. She then told me that I wasn't allowed to do any of the fun things on the trip, so I just stayed in my dorm room alone for the remainder of the time. I didn't mind – at least there were no new surprises and I knew my environment.

Environments could be such a problem for me and cause what I now understand to be sensory overload. On the school bus on the way home I was told to sit at the front with the teachers. It was meant to be a punishment for being disruptive, but I was secretly happy because it meant I could avoid the smell of sweat and lunchboxes which made me feel like my head was going to explode.

But, as I turned to look behind me, I saw that everyone else on the trip was smiling, laughing and enjoying themselves. Why couldn't I feel like that? Why was I so disconnected from my peers? Why couldn't I just fit in?

As a child and teenager, I didn't like myself very much. I spent so much of my time and energy just trying to fit in that I wasn't able to concentrate on anything else. I endlessly studied what other people said and did in different situations and I copied their actions and expressions, desperately hoping that it made me seem 'normal'. Of course the problem with this was that, despite my best efforts, I often came across as inauthentic. When I heard the other girls at school calling me 'fake' it only made me feel more miserable. Whatever I did, I just couldn't win.

But the thing that changed everything for me was discovering dance.

I remember going to my first dance class and watching the dance teacher as she stood in front of the room, showing us the steps and the choreography. I remember thinking, "This is amazing – there's somebody in front of me showing me exactly what I need to do".

I couldn't get the moves right straight away, and I wasn't brilliant to begin with, but the thing that made my heart sing was that lightbulb moment of realisation that life was better when people showed me what to do, step by step. That was the moment when the world really clicked for me.

The more I danced, the better I became, and the better I became, the more I learned to like myself. It was the point when I first felt fully connected with myself and I began to believe that I could learn to connect with others.

Becoming a dancer was the first time that I reinvented myself, but it certainly wasn't the last. After my knee injury and later, when I received my autism diagnosis, I reinvented myself as the UK's leading neurodiverse black female speaker. A large part of my journey to success has involved reframing the way I communicate with the world by developing a powerful personality to get my message across.

LIFE LESSON 4:

Reinvent yourself by creating a powerful personality

If you truly desire to achieve something you've never achieved before, you must be willing to become someone you've never been before. The essence of reinvention lies not in discarding your true self, but in shedding the limitations of who you think you are in favour of who you genuinely aspire to be. Throughout my career, I primarily saw myself as a dancer, a professional in every sense. I immersed myself in the dance world, working diligently to attain the peak of physical fitness, allowing me to perform at my absolute best.

This principle holds true across any career transition. Each time I've pivoted in my professional journey, I've faced the challenge and opportunity of reinvention. While this process can be intimidating, even overwhelming, it's crucial to recognize that you're not leaving behind your essence. Instead, you're carrying forward the best parts of your past self, harnessing those strengths to achieve new aspirations. Reinvention doesn't mean forgetting who you were; it means evolving into who you wish to become.

My journey in dance taught me this first-hand. Every step, every move, every performance bolstered my confidence. Dance served as a profound catalyst, illuminating the principle that dedication, consistent hard work, and repetition lead to mastery. This philosophy has been my guiding star, applicable in every sphere of life. Whenever I find myself in unfamiliar territory, I remind myself of the need for reinvention to align with my new goals.

But reinvention doesn't stop at personal mastery; it extends to working on a dynamic personality. A significant portion of our success hinges on our relationships, on how harmoniously we connect with others. Building strong, genuine bonds is pivotal to our progress. But to truly thrive in our relationships with others, we first need to develop a deep understanding and connection with ourselves. Self-awareness is a powerful process, enabling us to adapt, grow, and cultivate healthier relationships with those around us.

I worked hard to create a powerful personality – and it's something that I believe every person can begin to cultivate.

Wondering how you can reinvent yourself without losing who you are? Here are my five top tips:

1. **Focus on the positive**
   If you want to attract positive people, it stands to reason that you need to be positive yourself. Successful people never waste their energy grumbling, looking for the negative in things or pondering why they are so hard done by. It's time to keep your complaining in check.
2. **Become a great conversationalist**
   It's tempting to become so wrapped up in your own goals that all you talk about is yourself. Don't do it! If you want to build strong relationships with others, you need to become truly interested in them. You need to ask questions that make people feel seen, heard and validated and, crucially, you need to really listen to their answers. Never try to jump in and speak when someone else is talking – that only makes people feel uncomfortable.
   I always set myself a goal of finding out something new about someone every time I meet them, and I suggest that you do that too. As well as being a fun little challenge, it's a great way to build genuine connections and expand your own world views.
3. **Leave every room better than when you entered it**
   Whenever you meet anyone, whether they are a business contact, a client, a friend or a family member, your intention should be to make them feel better because they have spent time with you.
   Like the late, great Maya Angelou said, "I've learned that people will forget what you said, people will forget what you did, but people will never forget how you made them feel."
4. **Do 1% more than is expected of you**
   A great way to build relationships is by adding value. Always do exactly what you've said you'll do, but add a cherry on top as well. It's not about showing off or being extra – it's about being kind, helpful and human. This act alone sets you apart from others. Stay a little longer at work, do a little more than expected.

5. **Smile more**

Smiling is like nature's happy drug. When you smile at somebody it makes you feel good, and when a person smiles back it makes them feel good. Smiling costs nothing but is the easiest possible way to build a powerful personality. Get out there and do it today! It feels good to smile.

CHAPTER 5:

Finding light in the darkness of grief

It was a bright June day, but I had pulled the blinds down in my living room because I was too sad to deal with the sun. The kettle had just boiled, so I picked it up to make my tea. I was doing it on autopilot, my mind elsewhere, and as I poured the water, it sloshed out of the spout over the side of the kitchen counter and down onto my foot. As the scalding water hit my skin, I inhaled sharply, closed my eyes and winced.

And then I paused. I exhaled gently. I opened my eyes and I suddenly realised that the searing hot pain of the boiling water had been the only thing that had alleviated the overwhelming pain of the past few months. The worst pain I had ever experienced. The pain of losing my mum.

It may have only lasted for a moment, but the scalding water felt like a sweet relief.

****

Everyone says their mum is special. But my mum? Well, in my humble opinion, she was the best. Because the thing about my mum is she didn't give birth to me, but she loved me and protected me as fiercely as a lioness does her cub and, ultimately, she changed the course of my life.

Me and my mum

I was born Ifeoluwa Gloria Kuku to a Nigerian couple in 1984. They had come to London on student visas in the early 1980s. Towards the end of their fourth year here, my birth mother fell pregnant with me. She was only 21 years old, she had nothing, and her student visa was about to run out because she had just graduated so she needed to move back to Nigeria. I can't even begin to imagine how difficult the situation she found herself in must have been.

My birth mother wanted to give me the best life possible so, after a lot of thought, she decided to leave me in the UK when she and my birth father returned to Nigeria. She knew that if I stayed here, I could gain my British citizenship.

Initially I lived with my birth grandmother in Brixton in South London. But looking after an unexpected baby wasn't easy for her and she soon realised that she might not be able to cope in the long term. Around the same time that this was happening, three of my second cousins had been placed into foster care with a couple in Newport Pagnell. After discussing things, my mother and my grandmother decided to ask the couple if I could be placed with them as well so that I could grow up with my second cousins.

I was six weeks old and wearing a tiny yellow baby grow. Apparently, my birth mother and my grandmother took me to their house, asked my mum if they would look after me, and my mum looked at me, gave a big smile, and said, "We'll take her!"

My birth mother and my grandmother hugged my mum, and that was that. From that point onwards, Laura and Michael Barton became my parents, and I could not have been luckier.

Life in my mum and dad's house was a beautiful kind of chaos. As well as fostering my five second cousins, they also had three older children of their own as well as a granddaughter who lived with them. As far as we were concerned, we were all siblings. We were a team – we were one big, blended family and we all had each other's backs. Whether we were black or white, biological or non-biological children, my mum and dad loved us all unconditionally and treated us as their own.

Like any other family, we had our challenges. Space was at a premium, and both the living room and the conservatory were turned into bedrooms – and bedrooms were often fought over. We were forever waiting for our siblings to grow up and move out so we could get an upgrade. I shared a room with one of my sisters for many years until my brother went to uni, leaving me with my own room at long last. That was a day of celebration. Mealtimes were crazy, arguments were regular, and the laundry was never ending – but there was a lot of love in that house and my mum presided over it all.

My mum and dad decided to foster children because they had big hearts and they just wanted to help, so they just found a way to fit more children into their lives. My dad was an engineer and my mum was a seamstress. She was always so well put together, so she went out of her way to make sure we were too.

Me, Mum and Dad

As one of the very few black families in our area in the 1980s, everyone knew who my foster siblings and I were even if they didn't know our names. We stood out and, even though we had never asked to be on show, the fact was, we were on show a lot. My mum knew that, and I think she wanted to do whatever she could to stop us from being judged, so she always made sure we looked well turned-out in the most crisp and stylish clothes. Instilling us with high standards was her way of giving us one less thing to contend with.

Because there were always things to contend with. Like the day when I was playing out on the street with my sister and my friend Jenny from next door. We were all having fun tearing around and shrieking, when suddenly one of our neighbours – an old lady called Doreen with permed hair in a pink rinse – stepped out of her front door and shouted, "Go away, you little jungle puppets!"

I didn't really know what it meant, but I knew she had been looking at me when she shouted it, so I ran home to tell my mum. My mum listened to me repeating what Doreen had said. She nodded calmly, but her face was set in determination. She would not let it stand.

A few days later, she walked into the kitchen with her weekly shopping.

"Doreen won't be saying anything to you again," she said.

She then recounted the story of a show-down at the deli counter in the Co-op. Mum had spotted Doreen and called her out on her racism in front of a queue of old ladies and all the shop staff. My mum didn't mince her words and Doreen ended up scuttling off with a face as red as a tomato, and half a pound of Spam in her hand.

At the time, I was painfully embarrassed, but looking back I feel so proud. My mum didn't let anyone mess with her or her kids, and her fearlessness continues to inspire me every day in parenting my two boys.

As I grew up, my mum was there for me every step of the way. As soon as dance became a big part of my life, my mum became my biggest supporter.

Mum and Dad cheering me on from the audience

“Go on, Ife!” she would shout after every single performance, whether it was in our living room or at the dance class I went to with two of my sisters. By the time I’d left home and begun to pursue a career in dance, she was always by my side. When I appeared on the BBC show Dance X, she was there in the audience, beaming with pride.

Once I had a family of my own, my mum was the best Nanny. She came on holiday with us and fawned over my boys. The love was enormous.

My sons with my mum

I saw my biological mother a few times during my childhood – a couple of times while I was a little girl, and then once again when I was 17 when she was visiting the UK. I was shocked to discover how similar I looked to her.

Our faces were so alike, and we even moved in the same way. My birth mother was kind, but chatting to her felt like I was talking to a stranger.

Me and my birth mother in 1984

Me and my birth mother in 2023

After that whole experience when I was 17, time just rolled on.

In my early 20s, with access to smart phones, we started chatting on WhatsApp, and she'd drop me messages on the regular. She always rooted for me, sent prayers and scriptures my way, and she never missed a birthday message for me or the kids. She was a constant, quiet cheerleader in the background of my life.

Fast forward to May 2023 and, out of the blue, I got an invite to deliver a TEDx talk in Abuja, Nigeria. I couldn't turn it down. Not only was it an amazing gig, but it was also an opportunity to catch up with my birth mother. The last time I had seen her in the flesh was a whole 16 years ago in 2007, back before the boys were born.

My birth mother went all out in helping to sort out the arrangements to make sure I could transition from London to Abuja smoothly. She was all over it, understanding that the country and the culture were all pretty new to me.

We spent an incredible week together, and what hit me was how much she and my adoptive mum were cut from the same cloth – both of them generous, kind, selfless souls.

Being with her and seeing how we shared not just looks but also quirks, was mind-blowing. One time, I even half-joked about whether she'd ever thought about getting an autism diagnosis, given all the traits that I'd noticed in her. She responded with a puzzled "Huh?" But it was so good to see.

I came away from that week filled with gratitude. I was so grateful to my birth mother for being the amazing woman that she is, and for giving me life. I used to think that being adopted was a dark patch in my life, but looking back now, it's been the brightest light. I've been lucky enough to have two incredible mums – one who raised me, and one who brought me into this world. Both have loved me to bits.

Ultimately, though, my birth mother wasn't my mum. My mum was Laura Barton, and while we didn't look alike in any way, she was the woman who protected me, and shaped me into the person that I am today and for that, I will be forever grateful.

Me and my mum

****

Back in my kitchen in 2018, I stared down at my scalded foot and thought about how my life had been crumbling ever since my mum had died.

She had been diagnosed with a brain tumour in January, and died on 18 March – Mother's Day weekend. It was now June, and I was struggling to process everything that had happened.

I remembered the phone call I had received to say that Mum was nearing the end. I remembered racing over to her house in the car but arriving moments too late. I remember the guilt I felt at not visiting earlier.

I remembered sitting in the waiting room of the chapel of rest with all my siblings. I remembered the attendant coming in to tell us that my mum's body was ready to be viewed. As the attendant looked around, she was confused by the many black and white faces in the room, so she asked who everyone was.

My eldest brother pointed to himself and my mum's other two birth children and said, "She was our mum."

Then, pointing to the rest of us, he said, "And these are the foster children."

I know that he never meant it to sound so dismissive, but those few words crushed my heart and soul, and those of my foster siblings as well.

"She was our mum too!" I wanted to shout.

My mum had always treated all her children the same and made us feel like one big team, but now that she had gone, it seemed like we were being treated differently. If he didn't see us as real siblings, then who were we? Who did we belong to? I felt very alone and very confused. The only person who could have made me feel better was my mum, but she was no longer there.

The emotions that I had been experiencing over the past few weeks had been too much. The pain of knowing that I could no longer see or hug my mum was overwhelming and I had been self-medicating with drink. Getting the kids to school every morning was a struggle, I couldn't keep on top of anything and getting on with work felt impossible.

And here I was, standing in my kitchen, finding relief through the new pain of my scalded foot. The boiling water served as a temporary distraction, activating pain receptors in a different part of my brain and dulling the sense of grief. Up until then I had never understood why people self-harm, but it suddenly became clear to me: the temporary pain momentarily takes away your more permanent pain, and that can feel dangerously good.

I'm not ashamed to say that I felt a strong temptation to continue self-harming. However, as a coach, my intellectual mind quickly took over. I knew that my mum would hate to think of me hurting myself or letting my life collapse around me. She had rescued me as a baby to give me the opportunity to live a better life. She had shaped my future, been there for me in the bad times and cheered me on during the good times. I realised that my mum would want me to grab life by the horns and live fearlessly.

I decided that I couldn't handle my grief alone. I knew that the best way to deal with it would be to seek help so that I could take back control of my life. I remembered that the Macmillan nurses who had helped to look after my mum had told the family that we were entitled to bereavement support, so I decided to call Macmillan Cancer Support. As a result, I received ten free therapy sessions and it was one of the most transformative and cathartic experiences of my life. It gave me the opportunity to sit in the darkness and pour out my feelings to someone who was non-judgemental and share my truth in a way I never had before.

The therapy helped me to grow. It reminded me that we only have one life, so we have to go for it. That's how I've been living ever since, and I know that my mum would be proud of me.

I talk to my sister Mandy every day, and my dad is still here at 89 years old. Whenever we see a feather it reminds us that Mum is keeping an eye on us. Mum is our angel and it gives me comfort knowing this.

Me and my sister Mandy

Me and my dad

These days, whenever I achieve a new goal, launch a new project or step on a stage to deliver a TEDx talk, I can always hear my mum's voice in my head shouting, "Go on, Ife!"

TEDx

LIFE LESSON 5:

Never give up

Hopefully this book has shown you how it's always possible for you to overcome your challenges and transform your moments of darkness into moments of bright and brilliant light that allow you to shine like the star you are.

By this point I hope that you will have decided what you want from your life, identified someone who can show you how to get it, learned how to take control of your thoughts and discovered how you can reinvent yourself to achieve your success. Now all you need to do is keep going.

Stay persistent

Now that you have a plan, you need to stick with it through thick and thin. Times will get tough, your schedule will get busy, and there will be moments when you feel like you simply can't be bothered. But you must ignore those feelings and keep ploughing on regardless until you achieve your goal.

Sometimes your progress will feel frustratingly slow and you may begin to wonder whether any of your hard work is paying off. But, believe me, it is. In our fast-paced world, we all want instant results and learning to delay gratification is a challenge, but that's what you have to do. Remember, it takes more than one session in the gym to get a six pack – you only get one through boring, regular training. The same goes for your goals.

Every day, I want you to do something big or small that will move you closer to your goal. Make it a non-negotiable part of your life. If you need some motivation, just close your eyes and visualise how you will feel when you achieve your goal. All this work will be worth it.

I know how tempting it can be to sit on the sofa eating crisps, drinking wine, watching pointless television and feeling sorry for yourself. But I also know that doing these things won't contribute to my personal growth and it won't help me to achieve the financial freedom I'm aiming for. It won't contribute to building the spiritual or physical connections with the people that I love, and it certainly won't contribute towards making the world a better place.

Start where you are today

I want you to know that you can start to achieve your goals right here, right now. Don't wait until tomorrow, or Monday, or New Year's Day. Grab a pen and a piece of paper and write down three things that you could do today that will help move you to move closer to your goals … and then do that every single day for the rest of your life.

CONCLUSION:

Getting comfortable with the darkness

Now that you've come to the end of my book, there's one final thought that I want to leave you with:

Whenever you are in any challenging or painful moment, you need to intentionally take the time to sit in the dark.

I believe we all need to take ownership of our darkness rather than to ignore it, because when you suppress the pain that you feel it can consume you. Only by taking the time to pause, accept the darkness, feel the pain, and process what has happened to you can you start to make a plan for stepping into the light.

Once you've sat in the pain for long enough, that's the time to action **STEP 1 (Decide what you want)** and create a vision for how you are going to approach the rest of your life. The goal that you decide on will be your light – and that will be the thing that pulls you out of the darkness.

Like you've just read, I've been through a lot of periods of darkness in my life, but they have all been the moments that have made me. They have been the moments that have given me the time to develop a clear purpose. They will be the moments that will do the same for you.

You have greatness in you! Now it's time to own your shine. Grab hold of your light and use it to guide you along your journey.

You've got this! The world is just waiting for you to step into your light!

My truth

I am a work in progress. We all are. The darkness can descend upon any one of us at any given time. Over the past five years, particularly after the passing of my mum, I've been plunged into the depths of darkness twice. On both occasions, I didn't immediately recognise that I was in one of those 'sitting in the dark' moments. Sometimes, the darkness engulfs you when you least expect it, pulling you in, against all resistance.

Take 2020, for instance. The tragic murder of George Floyd. The event left me shaken to the core, prompting me to retreat to my room, hiding away from the world for two days. The trauma felt like every racist experience had opened up, I saw them as little paper cuts – my own analogy for racism. Each tiny paper cut, previously healed, was suddenly and violently reopened when I witnessed George Floyd's horrifying end. And in that moment, I felt I had no tools, no strategies to cope. I was bleeding out emotionally. So, I sought refuge in the dark until I could find my path to the light. Upon emerging, I took a significant step: I initiated a race conversation with my closest allies. That discourse, which we later shared on YouTube, reached 10,000 views, turning into one of the most transformative race dialogues I've ever participated in. It was a moment of reckoning, a time when I truly discovered my voice.

And then there was this year. Through introspection, I've come to realise that I handle professional rejection and failure well, but personal rejection? It's a completely different beast. It's my Achilles heel, that one chink in my armour. This vulnerability stems from a deep-seated pain, tracing back to my early days, when I was abandoned by my birth parents. The narrative I've constructed over the years might sound like I've made peace with that part of my past, but the truth is, on a cellular level, the trauma persists. The weight of that early rejection remains with me. It's a profound wound that, regardless of how much I evolve, never truly goes away. And so, when I confront those moments of overwhelming emotion, I've learned to pause, to ask: "Why do I feel this way?" Understanding and pinpointing the root of my pain helps me own it, rather than let it own me.

What I know for sure is that life will hand you its share of pain, trauma, disappointments, failures, and rejections. It's inevitable. But remember, the journey from darkness to light is about ownership. It's about working through, understanding, and then emerging on the other side. Every single one of us has the capacity to find the light in the shadows.

The work to uncover it? That's an inside job. With all my heart, I send you love and strength. The next time darkness pulls at you, always remember: your light is waiting, and you have the power to find it.

My boys Quincy and Quba

I dedicate this book to my family –
my husband Terrance and my sons, Quincy and Quba.